Twenty Steps to Your Turnaround

JEANNE SEVERE

WESTBOW
PRESS®
A DIVISION OF THOMAS NELSON
& ZONDERVAN

WestBow Press books may be ordered through booksellers or by contacting:

WestBow Press
A Division of Thomas Nelson & Zondervan
1663 Liberty Drive
Bloomington, IN 47403
www.westbowpress.com
844-714-3454

ISBN: 978-1-6642-4822-9 (sc)
ISBN: 978-1-6642-4821-2 (e)

Print information available on the last page.

WestBow Press rev. date: 11/02/2021

To my daughter and family:
Jason, my grandson
Ericka, my daughter
Samuel, my brother

Contents

Chapter 1

TAKE ACTION IN MOVING FORWARD TO DEFEAT YOUR SHORTCOMINGS

This book recounts the history of four hungry, filthy lepers who sat every day at the gate of Samaria, begging for food because there was a famine in the land. The story begins in 2 Kings 6:24–28. Mario was the leader of the group.

Mario told the group, "Today is a bad day. We have been sitting on the ground for the past four hours, and no one has given us even a piece of bread. If we continue to sit here, we all will die from hunger. What are we doing here? Quick—let's have a meeting. I have a great idea. What are we doing here? Listen to this thought that just came to my mind."

The other three friends got excited, and one asked Mario, "Are you going crazy or something? Tell us about it!"

Mario said, "All right, this is what we're going to do. I want us to do it as a group because there is power in numbers."

"Do what?" another asked. "What are you talking about?"

"Calm down," Mario told them. "I will tell you in a minute."

The three friends looked at Mario with their eyes wide open and their ears perked up, hoping to hear some good news.

These four lepers had been sitting every day at the gate of Samaria for several years, begging for food, money, or anything that passersby would give them for their survival.

Mario stood up and said, "Guys, I just had an insight. Life does not look good for any of us. We don't have two pennies to rub together. We have no hope, and we have no future. Think about that! We are four hungry, filthy, emaciated lepers, sitting at the city gate of Samaria, begging every day for our survival. I don't want to come to the end of my life and wonder about the things that I could have accomplished but never even tried. I don't want to be filled with doubts and uncertainty. All four of us don't have a place to live; we beg every day for our survival. We need counsel. We need to sit down and figure out how to improve our situation. Let's talk about this issue."

Mario sat down with a heavy sigh. "The problems we have are unpredictable," he said. "Some days we get something to eat; some days we don't. There is a famine in Samaria, so our welfare is not guaranteed on a daily basis."

"Staying hungry all day long and going to bed hungry is no joke!" one of the lepers said.

Mario nodded. "If we sit here, we will die. If we move back to town, where the famine is raging and there is no food, we also will die. But if we move forward, we will either get food or get killed. Will you all move forward with me?"

They all agreed with Mario.

"Let's not waste any time," Mario said. "Let's go to the camp of the Arameans and surrender to them. If we die, we die. If they capture us, we'll become slaves, but at least we'll have food to eat. I don't mind becoming a slave rather than starving to death."

"Let's do it! Let's go!" the other three shouted.

"The best option," Mario said, "is to get up, dust ourselves off, and move forward by faith. We don't know what the future holds for us, but I feel deeply in my spirit that the best is yet to come."

"We don't know what the future holds," one of the lepers said, "but we don't want to miss out on the blessing of the Lord."

"Let's give it a shot!" another added.

They all laughed with excitement, and the echo could be heard bouncing off a nearby mountain.

The Bible reads:

> Now there were four men with leprosy at the entrance of the city gate. They said to each other, "Why stay here until we die?" (2 Kings 7:3 NIV)

> If we say, We will enter into the city, then the famine *is* in the city, and we shall die there: and if we sit still here, we die also. Now therefore come, and let us fall unto the host of the Syrians: if they save us alive, we shall live; and if they kill us, we shall but die.

> And they rose up in the twilight, to go unto the camp of the Syrians: and when they were come to the uttermost part of the camp of Syria, behold, *there was* no man there. For the Lord had made the host of the Syrians to hear a noise of chariots, and a noise of horses, *even* the noise of a great host: and they said one to another, Lo, the king of Israel hath hired against us the kings of the Hittites, and the kings of the Egyptians, to come upon us.

> Wherefore they arose and fled in the twilight, and left their tents, and their horses, and their asses, even the camp as it *was*, and fled for their life. And when these lepers came to the uttermost part of the camp, they went into one tent, and did eat and drink, and carried thence silver, and gold, and raiment, and went and hid *it;* and came again, and entered into another tent, and carried thence *also*, and went and hid *it*. Then they said one to

another, We do not well: this day is a day of good tidings, and we hold our peace: if we tarry till the morning light, some mischief will come upon us: now therefore come, that we may go and tell the king's household.

So they came and called unto the porter of the city: and they told them, saying, We came to the camp of the Syrians, and, behold, *there was* no man there, neither voice of man, but horses tied, and asses tied, and the tents as they *were*. And he called the porters; and they told *it* to the king's house within.

And the king arose in the night, and said unto his servants, I will now shew you what the Syrians have done to us. They know that we *be* hungry; therefore are they gone out of the camp to hide themselves in the field, saying, When they come out of the city, we shall catch them alive, and get into the city. And one of his servants answered and said, Let some take, I pray thee, five of the horses that remain, which are left in the city, (behold, they *are* as all the multitude of Israel that are left in it: behold, *I say*, they *are* even as all the multitude of the Israelis that are consumed:) and let us send and see.

They took therefore two chariot horses; and the king sent after the host of the Syrians, saying, Go and see. And they went after them unto Jordan: and, lo, all the way *was* full of garments and vessels, which the Syrians had cast away in their haste. And the messengers returned, and told the king. And the people went out, and spoiled the tents of the Syrians. So a measure of fine flour was *sold* for a shekel, and two measures of barley for a shekel, according to the word of the LORD. (2 Kings 7:4–16 KJV)

The history on which I will focus is the four men with leprosy.

What Is Leprosy?

Leprosy is an infectious disease that causes severe, disfiguring skin sores and nerve damage in the arms, legs, and skin areas around your body. Leprosy has been around since ancient times. Outbreaks have affected people on every continent.

> But leprosy, also known as Hanson's disease, isn't that contagious. You can catch it only if you come into close and repeated contact with nose and mouth droplets from someone with untreated leprosy. Children are more likely to get leprosy than adults.
>
> Today, about 208,000 people worldwide are infected with leprosy, according to the World Health Organization, most of them in Africa and Asia. About 100 people are diagnosed with leprosy in the U.S. every year, mostly in the South, California, Hawaii, and some U.S. territories.

Leprosy Symptoms

> Leprosy primarily affects your skin and nerves outside your brain and spinal cord, called the peripheral nerves. It may also strike your eyes and the thin tissue lining the inside of your nose.
>
> The main symptom of leprosy is disfiguring skin sores, lumps, or bumps that don't go away after several weeks or months. The skin sores are pale-colored
> Nerve damage can lead to:
>
> - Loss of feeling in the arms and legs
> - Muscle weakness

It usually takes about 3 to 5 years for symptoms to appear after coming into contact with the bacteria that causes leprosy. Some people do not develop symptoms until 20 years later. The time between contact with the bacteria and the appearance of symptoms is called the incubation period. Leprosy's long incubation period makes it very difficult for doctors to determine when and where a person with leprosy got infected.

What Causes Leprosy?

Leprosy is caused by a slow-growing type of bacteria called *Mycobacterium leprae* (*M. leprae*)

Leprosy Diagnosis

If you have a skin sore that might be leprosy, the doctor will remove a small sample of it and send it to a lab to be examined. This is called a skin biopsy. Your doctor may also do a skin smear test. If you have paucibacillary leprosy, there won't be any bacteria in the test results. If you have multi bacillary leprosy, there will be.

Leprosy Treatment

Leprosy can be cured. In the last 2 decades, 16 million people with leprosy have been cured. The World Health Organization provides free treatment for all people with leprosy. (http://www. webmd.com/skin-problems-and-treatments/guide/ leprosy-symptoms-treatments-history)

Chapter 2

WHAT DOES LEPROSY REPRESENT IN THE BIBLE?

Leprosy was the scourge of the ancient world. Nothing evoked more fear, more dread, or more revulsion than the sight of these walking dead. That is what a leper was called, a walking dead man. The smell of his decaying flesh would announce his coming long before the tattered scraps of his clothing would be seen, or his raspy "Unclean! Unclean!" announcement he was required to declare, could be heard. The stumbling shuffle of toe less feet, the wandering of sightless eyes and the moan of a cheek less mouth, all pointed to Leprosy, this unseen attacker that slowly destroyed human bodies, and made the individual an untouchable to society. (https://www.christianity. com/jesus/birth-of-jesus/genealogy-and-jewish-heritage/how-is-leprosy-like-sin.html)

That was the physical description of leprosy, which these four lepers had to endure on a daily basis. Thank God, I never heard of that kind of disease on our shores.

What does leprosy represent in the Bible?

> Leprosy is a vivid and graphic physical picture of the spiritual defilement of sin. Sin is ugly, loathsome, incurable, and contaminating; it separates men from God and makes them outcasts. (http://www.christianity.com/jesus/birth-of-jesus/genealogy-and-jewish-heritage/how-is-leprosy-like-sin.html)

The Bible says:

> A man with leprosy came to him and begged him on his knees, If you are willing, you can make me clean." Jesus was indignant. He reached out his hand and touched the man. "I am willing," he said. "Be clean!" Immediately the leprosy left him and he was cleansed.
>
> Jesus sent him away at once with a strong warning: "See that you don't tell this to anyone. But go, show yourself to the priest and offer the sacrifices that Moses commanded for your cleansing, as a testimony to them." Instead he went out and began to talk freely, spreading the news. As a result, Jesus could no longer enter a town openly but stayed outside in lonely places. Yet the people still came to him from everywhere. (Mark 1:40–45 NIV)

When the untouchable was touched by Jesus, the leprosy was healed. Leprosy symbolized sin. When a sinner repents and confesses his sins to Jesus, Jesus forgives him for everything wrong that he ever did. The Bible says, "All have sin and come short of the glory of God" (Romans 3:23 KJV). Have you made peace with God in your heart? Jesus, the Son of God, left his throne in heaven and came down to earth. He suffered and died for us. When we accept him in our hearts, he gives us the privilege to be called children of God and to live with him in heaven forever and ever. If you want God to save you and give you eternal life, repeat the following prayer:

> Dear Lord Jesus, I know that I am a sinner, and I ask for Your forgiveness. I believe You died for my sins and rose from the dead. I turn from my sins and invite You to come into my heart and life. I want to trust and follow You as my Lord and Savior. Amen! (https://en.wikipedia.org/wiki/Sinner%27s_prayer)

Chapter 3

GOD CAN TURN YOUR
SITUATION AROUND

God can turn your situation around. The four lepers experienced lack of food; they were afraid, and they were frustrated with life. They were sick and unable to provide for their own needs. Their situation was bad.

This is what was happening in Samaria—plague with a severe famine: women were boiling their children for food, meaning that they were eating their own children. That was horrible. Practicing cannibalism was a crime punishable by the current law of the land.

Hungry citizens of Samaria were eating anything they could find. People ate disgusting things that I don't want to mention here.

People were selling donkeys' heads to eat for lots of money because there was a great famine in the land. These are the types of food that people ate to satisfy their hunger because they couldn't find real food to eat.

The land was dry and parched. There was no vegetation; there was no rain for several months. Gardens were not able to grow crops. That was a bad situation.

Feeling constantly hungry with a growling stomach is no joke.

Chapter 4

GOD IS YOUR PROVIDER; TRUST HIM

The people of Samaria ate all kinds of unhealthy food because there was a famine in Samaria. There was no rain for several months, and the land could not produce any food.

The following is an example of more unclean and unpalatable things they were eating. Let's read the story.

> The story begins in 2 Kings 6:24 with the siege of Samaria, Israel's capital city, and a tragic famine within the gates. Food and fuel prices had skyrocketed to the point that people were spending a fortune to eat unclean and unpalatable donkey heads (2 Kings 6:25).
>
> Beginning in 2 Kings 6:26, the cannibalism of the two mothers poignantly encapsulates Israel's problem. These two mothers had made a wicked pact with one another: to boil and eat their sons, first the one and then the other. (https://rezchurch. org/wp-content/uploads/From-Famine-to-Feast-2-Kings-7.pdf)

But after both mothers killed one son and ate him, the mother of the other child refused to kill her son. She took her son and hid him.

> So the mother whose son had been eaten cried out for help to the King of Israel. She [thought she] was seeking justice, but in fact what she sought was a great injustice: assistance in murdering and eating her neighbor's son.
>
> You need to know that this episode isn't only a macabre example of how bad things had gotten. (https://rezchurch.org/wp-content/uploads/From-Famine-to-Feast-2-Kings-7.pdf)

It seems to me that all hope was gone. This is ridiculous. I wonder what a grilled donkey head tasted like. The people of Samaria were eating donkey heads because of the famine; they couldn't find other food to eat. Life was so incredibly hard that women plotted together to eat each other's children so they could survive. It was very bad. The women committed a crime and murder in order to survive. That was a very bad situation. I can't believe I've heard such a report in my lifetime. Can you imagine going to the supermarket and seeing a donkey head with a price tag of $1,500? I probably would run away from that supermarket as soon as possible and never return there again.

Only God can change the situation by sending rain to the earth to renew nature and saturate the land with moisture so the land can produce fruits and vegetables to provide nourishment for the citizens of that land.

> Being hungry is never pleasant. In fact, hunger can inspire bizarre behavior in us humans. When we're hungry, we sometimes do foolish things, sometimes we get irritable, or worse, feel sorry for ourselves. (https://www.sermoncentral.com/sermons/

blessed-hunger-pangs-rob-woodrum-sermon-on-evangelism-the-lost-57450?page=1)

We feel ashamed of not having enough to eat. We blame ourselves for not saving enough money for rainy days. Hunger is not something that we desire.

When Jesus Christ said, "Blessed are they that do hunger and thirst after righteousness, for they shall be filled" (Matthew 5:6 NIV), he was inviting you to a spiritual banquet. The four lepers had a banquet prepared for them. The only thing they had to do was to get up, dust off, walk up, and show up. They filled their bellies and drank to their hearts' delight, and uncontrollable laughter filled the camp.

When God decides to bless you, he opens heaven on your behalf and pours out such a blessing that you will not be able to contain it. Trust God. He will open the door for you. All you have to do is receive it and say, "Thank you, Jesus."

Today, there are way too many people living on the edge, living too close to deception, too close to jumping right back into the past and all its failures. Let's bring all our cares to God, for he promises to take care of us.

Chapter 5

LESSONS LEARNED FROM THE FOUR LEPERS

Don't sit there until you die.

Don't stay where you are.

Take action.

Move forward.

Create a plan for success.

Chapter 6

GOD WILL BRING YOUR PLAN TO SUCCESS

Create a plan, even if you don't know what the result will be. God will bless your plan, even if it's not standard. The four lepers sat down and talked about what they wanted to do; then they got up and executed it. God was with them. God performed a miracle on their behalf—all the soldiers left the camp and start running for their lives because they were afraid of other enemies who came to attack them. That was God's strategy at work—to make room for the lepers to enjoy a good meal.

Then the LORD answered me and said:

"Write the vision
And make *it* plain on tablets,
That he may run who reads it.
For the vision *is* yet for an appointed time;
But at the end it will speak, and it will not lie.
Though it tarries, wait for it;
Because it will surely come,
It will not tarry. (Habakkuk 2:2–3 NIV)

God said to write the vision on a tablet, make it plain, and move forward.

Do not stay stuck in your situation.

> Stuck means being unable to move or being set in a particular position, place, or way of thinking; unable to change or get away from a situation.
>
> We can be trapped in a situation or even a way of thinking [for years]. This leaves us unable to see another way, to move or change. And it usually leads to repeating the same situation or thinking, over and over again. Most often, when we are stuck, it's because we are deeply attached to a story. (https://www.elairaflow.com/5-reasons-people-get-stuck-in-life-and-how-to-break-through/)

Do not stay stuck and die in your situation. God is faithful. He will give you a way to escape your situation when you trust in him.

Chapter 7

STUCK IN WHAT?

You might be stuck in depression, anxiety, or overwhelming stress. Don't be influenced by the naysayers or so-called friends—the friends who are jealous and won't do anything for themselves but will always find a way to criticize your progress.

There is hope in your situation. When you are stuck, surrounded by many problems, and you don't know what to do, lift up both arms to the heavens, surrender yourself to God, and say, as did the psalmist David,

> I will lift up mine eyes unto the hills, from whence cometh my help. My help cometh from the LORD, which made heaven and earth. (Psalm 121:1–2 NIV)

God will hear your prayer and make a way for you. Trust him; tell him your troubles. God will help you.

The lepers had a story that kept them stuck in their minds, but Mario, one of the lepers, had a vision that would revolutionize their lives forever. Mario sat down with the three men and had a conversation with them.

When you fall down and your backside touches rock bottom, that is the lowest you can go. The fastest way to get out of that mess is to look up and call on God for help. Ask him to come to your rescue, and confess your sin. Ask him to be your Savior.

God will answer with a still small voice. He will prompt in your spirit the right thing to do. God will answer, and you will experience a sudden feeling of joy, comfort, freedom in your spirit, and peace.

When God answers your prayers, an overwhelming love of God will conquer your soul. God will respond to the cry of your heart.

You must tell Jesus that you cannot carry your burdens alone. You must give all your troubles to him and accept him as your Lord and Savior. You must ask Jesus to forgive all your sins.

You must pray and worship the Lord. When you get up in the morning, thank God for giving you another day to live on this beautiful earth that he created for you to enjoy. Remember that God is always with you and always protecting you. Give him the praise that he deserves.

Chapter 8

STAND UP AND MOVE FORWARD

Mario, the leper who was more outspoken than his companions, told the three other lepers, "Come on; let's go. We need to move forward. We don't want to die here."

One of the three lepers answered, "I don't think I can make it. I am feeling so weak. I don't think I can walk that far."

"No worries, brother," Mario said. "We've got you! If you cannot walk, we will carry you. Right?"

The other two answered in unison, "Yes, we will help you."

Mario said, "Here is the last morsel of bread that we have saved. Eat it, and drink some water to replenish your strength." Mario then encouraged them by saying, "Come on! Together, we can do this! God is with us. We have nothing to fear!"

Chapter 9

GOD WILL RESCUE YOU FROM YOUR TROUBLES

Most of the remainder of 2 Kings 7:3–4 describes how God kept his word and came to Israel's rescue once more. It happened in two phases: first, with the four lepers who were not afraid but went to the Arameans' camp; and then, for the entire city of Samaria.

In 2 Kings 7:3–4, the four lepers sat down and discussed their situation. They decided that going over to the enemy camp would be their best chance for survival. The four courageous lepers mustered all their courage and walked toward the Arameans' camp, even though their legs and hands were shaking.

Their hearts were beating fast, but they were not afraid. They believed God would give them the strength to make the trip. The Bible says, "We walk by faith and not by sight" (2 Corinthians 5:7 NIV). They were encouraged by this verse to trust God, not their present circumstance.

Mario said, "Come on! Ready? Let's do it! Take one step at a time."

A journey of a thousand miles begins with a single step.
—Lao Tzu

Chapter 10

THE LEPERS' SONG

Mario, the leader, started to chant the lines of a song, and after each line he sang, the group echoed the words back to him. I imagine it went like this:

We are going to the enemy camp
We are starving, dirty, and thirsty
There, we will find some food
I am not staying here to die
Get up, clean up
Shake the dust off
Here we go
One step, two steps, three steps
And more

As we walk down the road
We know God is guiding us
We will fear no evil
God himself is here with us
We will conquer in his name
Come on! Get up, clean up

Shake the dust off
Here we go
One step, two steps, three steps
And more

The more the lepers sang the song, the more they were strengthened in their spirits. After a few hours, they finally made it to the camp.

At dusk they got up and went to the camp of the Arameans. When they reached the edge of the camp; to their surprise, no one was there. For the Lord had caused the Arameans to hear the sound of chariots and horses and a great army, so that they said to one another, "Look, the king of Israel has hired the Hittites and Egyptian kings to attack us!" (2 Kings 7:5 NIV)

It's amazing how God's plan works in our lives. While the lepers were painstakingly taking a breath to walk to the camp, God was busy on the other side of the mountain, kicking out the entire Aramean army to make room for the starving, emaciated, and thirsty lepers who needed food.

Hallelujah! God made provisions for his children. If you are hanging by a thread, God will take care of you. He will prepare a table for you in the presence of your enemies (Psalm 23:5).

The Aramean army was so scared that the men got up and fled into the dusk. They abandoned their tents, their chariots, and their highly equipped horses and donkeys; they also left gold and jewelry behind. They left the camp as it was, and they fled for their lives.

That was good news for the lepers who arrived at the camp that day and gathered the spoils left behind.

God fought the battle for the lepers and gave them victory. Amen!

God will also fight your battles and give you victory. God is the same yesterday, today, and forever. God never changes. What he did for others, he will do for you.

The men who had leprosy reached the Arameans' camp, but they found the enemy camp deserted. The Arameans had fled in fear of what they believed was a surprise attack by the Egyptians, but it was only the four lepers' footsteps that had made them flee. Think about it. The Lord multiplied the sound of the four lepers' footsteps. The Arameans thought a great army had come to invade their land to fight with them. The news spread across the camp. The Arameans were afraid for their lives. They fled on foot and left everything behind. They left the well-equipped horses, chariots, gold, silver, money, food, and wine.

My point is that God often accomplishes the impossible with the most improbable characters. In this case, he routed the Arameans with four starving men who looked like the walking dead—pale faces, emaciated, dusty, and thirsty—who just wanted some food.

When the lepers entered the tent, they saw everything they ever wanted—food, wine, coffee, tea, sandwiches, ice cream, pizza, cooked steaks, salads, exotic rice, roasted turkey, salad, hot dogs, chicken, pork, lasagna, breads, soups, cakes, tiramisu. Everything was at their disposal for free. They ate and drank to their hearts' delight.

While they were walking down the road in unity, worshiping and praising God, God was preparing a feast for them. God always make provisions for his children.

Believers in Christ, if you are going through tough times, don't worry. God said, "Fear not for I am with you" (Isaiah 41:10 NKJV).

> So do not fear, for I am with you; do not be dismayed, for I am your God. I will strengthen you and help you; I will uphold you with my righteous right hand. (Isaiah 41:10 NIV)

God is working behind the scenes to make all crooked places straight, and he will render the victory to you in such a way that will blow your mind. Trust him, continue to pray, and worship him. Don't give up.

How to Shake Up the Dust in Our Lives Today

These are a few of the "dusts" that we experience while we live on earth: failure, rejection, anger, discouragement, anxiety, hatred, doubt. If these negative qualities have been part of your life, you must rise up and shake them off. These negative feelings keep you in bondage. You must get rid of them to regain your freedom and move on with your life. Don't let any mental burden crush you; give it to Jesus.

Shake off any failure that assails you, and move on with your life. Change the way you think.

Repeat the following positive affirmations daily:

> Today, I accept you, Jesus, into my life. Jesus is my Lord and Savior. Jesus loves me. Jesus cares for me. I believe in God, my Father. I believe in Jesus, my redeemer. I believe in the Holy Spirit, my helper. I shake off the dust of my failures. I am strong. I am moving on. I will reach my destination safely with the help of God. I meditate on God's Word every day. I am obedient to God. I talk to God every day. I repent of my sins. I forgive people who offend me. I will not allow words of fear, curses, or doubt to proceed from my mouth.

Be obedient to God's Word. When you abide in Christ, you will receive the gift of the Holy Spirit that will enable you to bear spiritual fruits. These are the fruits that you will produce.

But the fruit of the Spirit is love, joy, peace, forbearance, kindness, goodness, faithfulness, gentleness and self-control. Against such things there is no law. (Galatians 5:22–23 NIV)

As you continue your journey with your heavenly Father, remember one thing: Jesus loves you, and he forgives all your sins. Find a good Bible-believing church to teach you the Word of God, a church that will encourage you in your walk of faith. Read the Bible every day, starting with the book of John 1–21 (New Testament). Be obedient to God's Word. As you surrender yourself to God's Word, his presence will be with you. He will keep you and guard you in all your ways.

Chapter 11

THIS IS A DAY OF GOOD NEWS

Second Kings 7:8–12 continues the story of the four lepers:

> The lepers feasted and plundered the camp of the Arameans, but it wasn't long before they felt convicted and said, "We aren't doing right. This is a day of good news." So they repented and then resolved to share the gospel (good news) with everyone else by going to tell the king. When they did, however, the apostate king still would not believe [their story]. He thought it was a trap (7:12).
>
> Thankfully his servants had the good sense to at least consider whether the good news of the lepers might also be good news for them too. (https://rezchurch.org/wp-content/uploads/From-Famine-to-Feast-2-Kings-7.pdf)

So the king granted them permission to check it out. The king of Samaria consented to sending out a group of officers to search the Arameans' camp, and they eventually confirmed the good news that the lepers had told the king.

The good news spread like wildfire to the Samarian citizens. By the next morning, the whole city had gone to feast and gather the spoils; they plundered the camp that the Aramean army had left behind. Our great God had won the victory. Glory to his name!

The good news had spread throughout Samaria, throughout the whole city, and everyone went to the Aramean camp to get some food to feed themselves and their families.

After we are saved, we need to tell other people about Jesus so they too will come to know Jesus as their Savior.

Chapter 12

GOD WILL ALWAYS COME THROUGH FOR HIS CHILDREN

What situation keeps you bound?

Remember always that God is a good God. God loves you. God wants to break the chains that bind you and set you free. He wants you to live a life of peace, joy, love, and prosperity.

He wants you to follow his ways. He wants you to share his love and goodness with others.

He cares for you.

Trust in the Lord with all your heart.

God intervened in the four lepers' situation. He lifted them out of the pit of desperation and led them to a feast fit for a king. The mess that God pulled them out of became a message that was reported to the king of Samaria. The good news eventually spread to the whole city.

The good news was, "There is food in the Aramean camp. If you can make it there, your belly will be full, and your thirst will be quenched."

The next morning at the break of dawn, the entire city traveled to the enemy camp. When they arrived there, they ate and drank and then gathered the leftovers, including clothes, jewelry, money, and lots of amenities. Then the people went back home, rejoicing and carrying the spoils that they had gathered from the camp. The lepers had saved the entire city from destruction.

The Bible says:

> The LORD is my shepherd; I shall not want. He maketh me to lie down in green pastures: he leadeth me beside the still waters. He restoreth my soul: he leadeth me in the paths of righteousness for his name's sake. (Psalm 23:1–3 KJV)

God leads his children beside still waters. He leads us to a place of peace and rest.

He makes us lie down in green pastures. God refreshes our souls and leads us to abundant life.

Trust the Lord, and in all your ways, acknowledge him, and he will direct your path.

Psalm 40:1–3 tells us that King David trusted in the Word of the Lord. When he waited patiently for the Lord, God inclined and heard his cry. God lifted him up out of the pit, set his feet upon the rock, and made his footsteps firm. As a result, King David sang a new song.

Chapter 13

TRUST GOD AND
MOVE FORWARD

Trust in the Word of the Lord, and wait patiently for him. He will set your feet upon the rock, and you will sing a new song.

If you are experiencing some kind of setback, either financial or emotional difficulties; if you are hanging by a thread, call on Jesus. He can help you turn your situation around. You can pray this simple prayer and invite God to come in and take residence in your life:

> Dear Lord Jesus, I know that I am a sinner, and I ask for Your forgiveness. I believe You died for my sins and rose from the dead. I turn from my sins and invite You to come into my heart and life. I want to trust and follow You as my Lord and Savior. Amen! (https://en.wikipedia.org/wiki/Sinner%27s_prayer)

Whatever situation you are going through, I encourage you to stand up, shake the chains of whatever tied you up, dust yourself off, look up to God, and move forward. God is waiting for your call. Give God something to work with. Whatever the problem is, God can handle it.

God loves us. He still is looking for ways to satisfy our hunger and needs. Don't hesitate to call on God. He is waiting on you. Jesus is on the line; tell him what you want.

God cares for you. He made provisions for the lepers; he will make provisions for you.

The Importance of Worshipping God in Our Lives

When we worship God, we pay homage to him for what he has done in our lives. Every day, God works miracles in our lives; whether or not we see the miracles is another story. God works wonders behind the scenes in our lives each day. It looks like a Broadway show production. All the cast members rehearse behind the scenes. They rehearse many hours, days, and months until everything is done perfectly. Then, at the appointed day and time, the audience appears and—*voilà!*—with the blaring of the trumpets, the beating of the drums, the multicolored lights, and the melodious sound of the piano, the audience rises to their feet, shouting and clapping with all their might. An exuberant joy fills the theater. When the curtain comes down at the end of the show, everyone laughs and agrees with each other that they just experienced a spectacular show on Broadway! They comment that the show was magnificent!

God worked for the four lepers behind the scenes. They mustered their courage by faith, not knowing what the future held for them, and walked to the enemy camp, where God already had prepared a banquet for them. The four lepers were not afraid to go to Samaria, to the enemy camp, and enjoy the feast that was left there, untouched, because God had made a way for them. Hallelujah!

A Psalm of David

The Lord is my shepherd; I shall not want. He maketh me to lie down in green pastures: he leadeth me beside the still waters. He restoreth my soul: he leadeth me in the paths of righteousness for his name's sake. Yea Though I walk through the valley of the shadow of death I will fear no evil for thou art with me. Thy rod and thy staff they comfort me. Thou preparest a table before me in the presence of my enemies Thou anointed my head with oil Surely goodness and mercy shall follow me all the days of my life and I will dwell in the house of the Lord forever and ever (Psalm 23:1–6 KJV)

We wonder what God has in store for us when we walk by faith and not by sight. In the same way that God made provisions for the four lepers, he will take care of us too. This is how God works. In spite of the lepers' pain, suffering, and rejection by society—they were marginalized because they had awful, disgusting sores on their bodies—God had mercy on them. God provided succulent food to strengthen their bodies.

According to Psalm 23:1–6, the lepers would gratefully say, "The Lord is my shepherd. I shall not want." In order for the lepers to move forward to become children of God, they needed to get rid of fear and step forward toward their destiny.

God made them lie down in green pasture. This is a place where hunger and thirst are satisfied. This is the place where God made the provision of sustenance, security, and serenity for them.

He led them beside the still waters. "Still waters" can be translated as "waters of rest." Yet we can see there is a change in what the sheep are doing, in that they are no longer lying down; instead, they are following the shepherd to the still waters where they can drink.

Right away, we can see from this description that the provision of refreshment for the sheep is the responsibility of the Shepherd. The appreciation of this reality should be of great comfort to his sheep because they know what kind of shepherd he is. If he was indifferent to them, then they would have no reason for comfort and for having a sense of anticipation or of security. But since they know what he is like, they have every reason to expect him to provide spiritual refreshment in calm locations for them.

The Lord gives peace and contentment in the mind to those who follow him. We are blessed with the green pastures of the provisions that he made for us. Let us make time to enjoy God's provision, but let us abide in them. The consolations of the Holy Spirit are the still waters by which the saints are led; the streams that flow from the fountain of living waters.

How refreshing, when we follow the leading of the Holy Spirit, to be led by the still waters of comfort, peace, and lying down in green pastures.

He restoreth my soul.

We hear the Lord condemning the shepherds of Israel. The Bible says in Ezekiel 34:4–16 that part of their guilt is that they have not brought back the sheep that have strayed (v. 4). When the Lord, later in the passage, states that he himself will be their shepherd, he says, in part, that he will bring back the sheep that have strayed (v. 16). There's our connection. We tend to see the sheep lying peacefully in the meadow, and we forget that sheep are contrary animals. They get up. They walk around. They stray. It is the task of the shepherd to bring them back. In the psalm, then, we see the shepherd, active, going after those sheep that have strayed, bringing them back to the flock. And we are comforted, knowing that our Good Shepherd will not allow us to stray too far. He will search us out and bring us back to the flock.

> For God so loved the world, that he gave his only begotten Son, that whosoever believeth in him should not perish, but have everlasting life. (John 3:16 NIV)

Since God gave his only begotten Son, that whosoever believes in him will not perish but have everlasting life, what can we give him in return? We give him our hearts; we serve and worship him. We live our lives to please him. We obey his Word. We spend time with him daily with our devotion and prayer.

Chapter 14

ASK GOD TO HELP YOU, AND HE WILL

Are you falling into temptation? Have you committed secret sin that nobody's knows about, like smoking, drinking alcohol, fornicating, or being addicted to drugs?

God is here to help you. His arms are extended toward you. God said to you, "Come unto me, ye who are heavily loaded, and I will give you rest."

> Then Jesus said, "Come to me, all of you who are weary and carry heavy burdens, and I will give you rest." (Matthew 11:28 NLT)

Jesus invites us to put our burdens down. Take some deep breaths. Inhale, exhale, and let it go.

> Give your burdens to the Lord, and he will take care of you. (Psalm 55:22 NIV)

Give your burdens to the Lord, and he will take care of you.

"When we give something to God, it feels wonderful because we are essentially giving the burden, the worries, and the cares of that thing over to Him" (https://dashingdish.com/blog/dashing-devotional-give-it-to-god-and-leave-it-there).

> We often experience unnecessary anxiety and burdens that we were never meant to carry. He showed her that this occurs when we bring something to God through prayer, but we ultimately end up 'taking it back'.
>
> When we give something to God, it feels wonderful because we are essentially giving the burden, worries, and cares of that thing over to Him.
>
> We are doing what Philippians 4:6 instructs us to do which is to, "Not be anxious about anything, but in everything, by prayer and petition, with thanksgiving, present your requests to God." And when we do this, we feel an overwhelming peace knowing that it is in His hands, which is what the next verse explains will happen … "And the peace of God, which transcends all understanding, will guard your hearts and your minds in Christ Jesus."
>
> The problem lies however, when we 'take back' that thing that we gave to Him in the first place. Whether it be taking back control of something we surrendered to Him, trying to take care of ourselves in an area, try to figure out our own way, when we initially asked for His direction … *All of these things will cause us to take back the very thing that we gave to God.* (https://dashingdish.com/blog/dashing-devotional-give-it-to-god-and-leave-it-there#:~:text=During%20her%20devotional%20time%2C%20God,up%20'taking%20it%20back')

Martha, a friend of mine, was planning her wedding. This was an overwhelming task, and she needed some help.

> She was in charge over all of the planning and delegating. She had so much on her plate with planning [the event] and working full time as a [registered nurse] that she suddenly found herself getting somewhat overwhelmed as the [wedding] date drew closer. However, when she started delegating tasks to people that she knew and trusted, she suddenly felt a huge weight taken off, and that the tasks she was responsible for were manageable.
>
> God showed her that this action of 'delegating tasks to others' was similar to giving things over to Him. When she gave things to Him that He promised to take care of (financial provision, protection, direction, just to name a few), then she could do her 'part' with ease and confidence knowing that He was taking care of His part. When she asked Him for something, or gave something over to Him, she was essentially trusting Him with that area of her life, and she didn't need to worry about if it would 'get done' or not. She simply had to trust that it was taken care of, and not give it a second thought.
>
> Then God spoke to her and said, 'Now what if you had taken back some of those tasks that you had previously delegated to people ... how would it have made you feel?' [Martha] replied, 'Burdened and overwhelmed'. God replied, 'You see, in life, whenever you are feeling overwhelmed or burdened by something, that is essentially what is happening! Every time you give something to me, and then take it back, you are taking on more than you

can handle, because you were never meant to do everything alone! You do your part, and give me what I already promised that I would take care of, and you will be able to manage you part with ease knowing that I am taking care of the rest!' (https:// dashingdish.com/blog/dashing-devotional-give-it-to-god-and-leave-it-there#:~:text=During%20 her%20devotional%20time%2C%20God,up%20 'taking%20it%20back'.)

The first and most important step in giving something to God and leaving it there, is to trust Him to take care of what He has promised to take care of. This trust can be developed in many different ways … But I have found there a few key ways that really stand out through the illustration God gave [my friend].

The people that my [friend] delegated tasks to for the [wedding planning] were people that she knew, loved, and therefore trusted. She knew that they were capable of the task, and that when they said they would take care of it, that it would get done. She never had to worry or have a second thought about if they would actually do what they promised, because she trusted their word.

We can get to that same place with God by understanding how much He cares for us, and loves us. If you don't feel like you have ever had a true revelation of His great love for you, that is certainly the first step in trusting Him. All you have to do is simply ask the Lord to reveal His great love for you … I can promise that He wants to show you even more than you want Him to!

Also, you have to know His promises to you. Take the area of finances for example, if you don't know that He promised to provide all of your needs (Philippians 4:19). ["And my God will meet all your needs according to the riches of his glory in Christ Jesus"]; then you will never know that is something He told you that He would do, so you won't really know if you can hand that over to Him, and trust Him with it. (https://dashingdish.com/ blog/dashing-devotional-give-it-to-god-and-leave-it-there#:~:text=During%20her%20devotional%20time%2C%20God,up%20'taking%20it%20back'.)

Through this revelation, God showed my [friend Martha] that every time we start to feel burdened, anxious, or overwhelmed by something in our lives, it is essentially because we haven't totally given it over to Him in the first place, or if we have, we have tried to take it back into our control. This action will always lead us to feelings of heaviness, because He never designed us to take on what He has promised to care for. (https://dashingdish.com/ blog/dashing-devotional-give-it-to-god-and-leave-it-there)

Jesus said,

Come unto me, all ye that labor and are heavy laden, and I will give you rest. Take my yoke upon you, and learn of me; for I am meek and lowly in heart: and ye shall find rest unto your souls. For my yoke is easy, and my burden is light. (Matthew 11:28–30 KJV)

This one scripture alone could answer all the problems in the world. Think about what could happen if everybody dropped their cares, their concerns, their fears, their failures, and their sins at the foot of the cross and let them go, meaning they would come to Jesus, pray to him, talk to him, and tell him about all their problems and ask forgiveness of their sins. They would live his presence, refreshed by God's mighty presence, as born-again children of the King. Becoming a child of God is about accepting God's gift, not earning salvation through works. You can use the following prayer to tell God that you want to accept Jesus Christ as your Savior:

> Dear God, I realize I am a sinner and could never reach heaven by my own good deeds. I want to become part of your family, and you have provided a way for me to become your child. Right now, I place my faith in Jesus Christ as God's Son, who died for my sins and rose from the dead to give me eternal life. Please forgive me of my sins and help me to live for you. Thank you for accepting me and giving me eternal life.
> Amen.

John the apostle proclaimed this; Matthew, Mark, and Luke proclaimed this. Today, I stand before you and proclaim that salvation is by coming to Jesus Christ and him only. To attempt salvation from any other manner will not save your soul, and therefore, you will not spend eternity with God in heaven.

Heaven is the ultimate place we want to go to after we die in Christ. Don't miss it!

> It would solve the failures in the lives of every person who turns back from following God. Coming to the Lord will bring victory in any person's life. This is

the loving Savior, speaking to each of us present today—He beckons us to Him.

"Come" means to leave what you are doing and start doing what the Lord bids you to do.

Come ... An invitation for rest. Freedom from all the cares of the world that surround a person who is trying to live for Christ.

Come—has a reward with it. By coming we receive all the Lord offers.

"Come"—indicates a move toward the Lord. You are coming to where He is—or where He wants you to be.

"Come"—there is no stipulation as to who can come. Anyone may come. The wealthy, the poor, the famous, the peasant. (https://www.sermoncentral. com/sermons/come-unto-me-ivan-casteel-sermon-on-discipleship-121782?page=1&wc=800)

At the foot of the cross, we are one; the invitation is given to all.

Would you like to get rid of your baggage, your anxiety, your fears and pain that have crippled your body for years? Do you want some relief from your failures?

Come to Jesus right now. His arms are open wide to receive you. The Lord says,

"Come unto me ..."

"Me" is Christ Jesus—the Son of God. The same person that said, "I am the way, the truth, and the life [no man cometh into the father, but by me" (John 14:6 KJV)].

(https://www.sermoncentral.com/sermons/ come-unto-me-ivan-casteel-sermon-on-discipleship-121782?page=1&wc=800)

The Bible says, "All that the Father give me shall come to me; and him that cometh to me I will in no wise cast out" (John 6:37 KJV). It's comforting to know that God will not kick us out, no matter how much we mess up. We have to repent from what we've done wrong. We must go to God to confess our sins, and God will forgive us.

> The Lord invites each person to come to Him for salvation.
>
> "Come" is for any person who wants to be saved. There is no limitation on who can be saved. "Whosoever believeth on Him shall be saved."
>
> "Come" is inclusive. It includes any and all who will come.
>
> "Come" is conclusive. He is the Author and finisher of our faith.
>
> "Come" is exclusive—It rules out any other method of salvation other than in Christ Jesus.
>
> "Come unto me" includes you if you accept—it rules you out if you reject—there is no other One to go to for salvation.
>
> Salvation is eternal life for all believers.
>
> You can probably remember when you were carrying your load of sin—there was no relief— no place to lay the burden down. Jesus so tenderly calls for all to "come" for cleansing—"come" and be made whole.
>
> This is so basic that it almost seems useless to say it again, but our command is to tell it over and over again.
>
> Salvation Is In Jesus Christ Only. (https://www.sermoncentral.com/sermons/come-unto-me-ivan-casteel-sermon-on-discipleship-121782?page=1&wc=800)

Chapter 15

LEARN AND BELIEVE THE WORD GOD TO TURN YOUR SITUATION AROUND

The Lord said, "Take my yoke upon you and learn of me" (Matthew 11:29 KJV). How do we learn of God?

"Take my yoke upon you." The yoke has many implications. The first thing that learning from Jesus means is bringing under control our passions and desires for the immoral and ungodly practices of the world. The nature of our culture makes the desires of the flesh so accessible that immorality is rampant and almost totally acceptable.

The yoke that draws to holy living often seems oppressive to the young and spiritually immature, but Jesus says the yoke is easy. In perspective the yoke is easy because it brings none of the guilt and suffering that comes with fleshly, immoral actions.

Further consideration of the yoke reminds me that it forces us to address our "stubborn hearts."

That phrase is used to describe the people Jesus addressed in Mark 3. (https://christianchronicle. org/meditation-to-understand-take-my-yoke-upon-you-and-learn-from-me)

Mark 3:1 tells us, "And [Jesus] entered again into the synagogue; and there was a man there which had a withered hand."

Another time Jesus went into the synagogue, and a man with a shriveled hand was there. Some of them were looking for a reason to accuse Jesus, so they watched him closely to see if he would heal him on the Sabbath. Jesus said to the man with the shriveled hand, "Stand up in front of everyone." Then Jesus asked them, "Which is lawful on the Sabbath: to do good or to do evil, to save life or to kill?" But they remained silent.

He looked around at them in anger and, deeply distressed at their stubborn hearts, said to the man, "Stretch out your hand." He stretched it out, and his hand was completely restored. Then the Pharisees went out and began to plot with the Herodians how they might kill Jesus.

Crowds Follow Jesus

Jesus withdrew with his disciples to the lake, and a large crowd from Galilee followed. When they heard about all he was doing, many people came to him from Judea, Jerusalem, Idumea, and the regions across the Jordan and around Tyre and Sidon. (Mark 3:1–8 NIV)

Do you want to be healed?

Come forward. Jesus had called attention to the man with a withered hand, a man in the synagogue, but the people were ready to condemn Jesus for healing on the Sabbath. God performed a miracle for the man; his hand was healed on the Sabbath day. The Pharisees and the Herodians got mad at Jesus because of this miracle. They thought of ways to hurt him.

> Again he entered the synagogue, and a man was there who had a withered hand. They watched him to see whether he would cure him on the sabbath, so that they might accuse him. And he said to the man who had the withered hand, "Come forward." Then he said to them, "Is it lawful to do good or to do harm on the sabbath, to save life or to kill?" But they were silent. He looked around at them with anger; he was grieved at their hardness of heart and said to the man, "Stretch out your hand." He stretched it out, and his hand was restored. The Pharisees went out and immediately conspired with the Herodians against him, how to destroy him. (Mark 3:1–6 NRSV)

Jesus was God. He had all the power to do all kinds of miracles. He was always being "scrutinized" by these groups of people—the Pharisees, the Sadducees, and the Herodians—who plotted ways to destroy him.

However, the man with withered hand was happy and blessed to receive his healing. He went home rejoicing and praising God.

> Most of us have stubborn hearts that sometimes resist the power of God. We are often confined by our traditions or our private interpretations of Scripture. Wearing the yoke of Jesus, we can manage our stubborn hearts so that we are open to

see God at work in our lives and in our world. It helps us cast aside whatever keeps us from knowing God. (https://christianchronicle.org/meditation-to-understand-take-my-yoke-upon-you-and-learn-from-me/)

The yoke of Jesus is all about heart and mind. It helps shape us in the image of Jesus so that we become meek and gentle in all our dealings. It equips us to deal with egos that drive us to all kinds of excesses. It helps us bring every thought and every action under the control of Jesus. It helps us love spiritual things more than we love the world. When we first put on the yoke, it is strangely uncomfortable and disturbing. But as time passes it begins to feel natural until it eventually seems to be a part of us that we could not function without.

The yoke of Jesus is never forced on us. We must make the decision to put on that yoke. That decision is the first step to surrendering our will, our control to a higher power. We make the decision, but the process of assuming the full weight of the yoke often takes a long time. (https://christianchronicle. org/meditation-to-understand-take-my-yoke-upon-you-and-learn-from-me/)

I made the decision to accept Jesus into my heart as my Lord and Savior when I was five years old.

The full significance of that decision is still registering with me. It became a more important decision every day throughout my life as I became an adult, [a wife, a mother of my daughter, a medica] professional educator.

Every event in my life has made me more aware of the [easy] yoke [of Jesus in my life] and its power over me to transform the way I have dealt with responsibilities [handed to me, to show Jesus in everything I do]. (https://christianchronicle.org/meditation-to-understand-take-my-yoke-upon-you-and-learn-from-me)

Chapter 16

TAKE THESE STEPS TO MOVE FORWARD

You have come to terms with the realization that there is something in your life that no longer fits, and you are ready to move beyond it. You are realizing not only that, your job, relationship, situation, or behavior has become stagnant and is no longer benefiting you, but resisting the ending is more painful than giving in and surrendering or letting go. You are ready to move forward but are afraid of what that entails. (https://www.huffpost.com/entry/5-ways-to-make-a-transiti_b_11234240)

Let's examine the steps to help you move with confidence, faith, peace, and ease to your destination, with almighty God on your side.

The first step is acceptance in moving forward to defeat your shortcomings.

Accept the realization that what you currently have is no longer satisfactory, that you are wanting something different, and that you are ready for it.

Take time to accept this and allow this knowingness to sink in. This first step tends to be the scariest because it means there will be change, and change brings vulnerability and discomfort. (https://www. huffpost.com/entry/5-ways-to-make-a-transiti_b_ 11234240)

You just have to step up and move on, although you don't know what the future holds, but you know there is something good waiting for you when you arm yourself with courage and move on with your life. Brighter tomorrows are waiting to embrace you and turn your missteps into opportunity.

Chapter 17

SPEAK POSITIVE THOUGHTS TO YOURSELF

"Change the thoughts that materialized the situation you were in. Transform and elevate thoughts that were working against you" (https://www.huffpost.com/entry/5-ways-to-make-a-transiti_b_ 11234240). Change negative thoughts into positive and optimistic thoughts. Watch your words; speak positive thoughts to yourself. Don't say, "I am not good at anything," or "I can never accomplish that."

> If you are moving forward from an unhealthy relationship and think that you will not find better or anyone else who will love you, change your thoughts to create a different attitude and a different outcome, such as, "I deserve someone who will love and appreciate me," or "I am confident I will find the perfect person for me." (https://www. huffpost.com/entry/5-ways-to-make-a-transiti_b_ 11234240)

Pray to God to bring the right person into your life. Remain positive, and trust the Lord. He will bring it to pass.

The Bible says,

> Trust in the LORD with all your heart,
> And lean not on your own understanding;
> In all your ways acknowledge Him,
> And He shall direct your paths. (Proverbs 3:5–6 KJV)

Break through limitations and barriers.

> Spiritual limitation—Isaiah 6v1—The Prophet's vision of God had been limited until the year that King Uzziah died. (https://www.daughtersofdestiny-ng.org/sermon/breaking-out-of-limitations/)

> The nation's prosperity under Uzziah was considered to have been a result of the king's fidelity to Yahweh. According to the biblical record, Uzziah's strength caused him to become proud, which led to his destruction. (https://www.britannica.com/biography/Uzziah)

> Fear—Fear can also limit a Christian from achieving or maximizing his potential. [The Bible said in] 2 Tim 1v7 here we can see that fear is a spirit, the NIV calls fear a spirit of timidity.
>   Limitation of the mind (Thinking)—In Numbers 13 when the children of Israel went to spy the land 10 out of 12 were limited in their thoughts and perceived themselves as grasshoppers. Thank God for Joshua and Caleb that were not negative or limited in their thinking. (https://www.daughtersofdestiny-ng.org/sermon/breaking-out-of-limitations/)

And the LORD spake unto Moses, saying,

> Send thou men, that they may search the land
> of Canaan, which I give unto the children of Israel:
> of every tribe of their fathers shall ye send a man,
> every one a ruler among them.
>
> And Moses by the commandment of the LORD
> sent them from the wilderness of Paran: all those
> men were heads of the children of Israel.
>
> And these were their names: of the tribe of
> Reuben, Shammua the son of Zaccur.
>
> Of the tribe of Simeon, Shaphat the son of Hori.
>
> Of the tribe of Judah, Caleb the son of Jephunneh.
>
> Of the tribe of Issachar, Igal the son of Joseph
>
> Of the tribe of Ephraim, Oshea the son of Nun.
>
> Of the tribe of Benjamin, Palti the son of Raphu.
>
> Of the tribe of Zebulun, Gaddiel the son of
> Sodi.
>
> Of the tribe of Joseph, namely, of the tribe of
> Manasseh, Gaddi the son of Susi.
>
> Of the tribe of Dan, Ammiel the son of Gemalli.
>
> Of the tribe of Asher, Sethur the son of Michael.
>
> Of the tribe of Naphtali, Nahbi the son of
> Vophsi.
>
> Of the tribe of Gad, Geuel the son of Machi.
>
> These are the names of the men which Moses
> sent to spy out the land. And Moses called Oshea
> the son of Nun Jehoshua.
>
> And Moses sent them to spy out the land of
> Canaan, and said unto them, Get you up this way
> southward, and go up into the mountain:
>
> And see the land, what it is, and the people that
> dwelleth therein, whether they be strong or weak,
> few or many;

And what the land is that they dwell in, whether it be good or bad; and what cities they be that they dwell in, whether in tents, or in strong holds;

And what the land is, whether it be fat or lean, whether there be wood therein, or not. And be ye of good courage, and bring of the fruit of the land. Now the time was the time of the first ripe grapes.

So they went up, and searched the land from the wilderness of Zin unto Rehob, as men come to Hamath.

And they ascended by the south, and came unto Hebron; where Ahiman, Sheshai, and Talmai, the children of Anak, were. (Now Hebron was built seven years before Zoan in Egypt.)

And they came unto the brook of Eshcol, and cut down from thence a branch with one cluster of grapes, and they bare it between two upon a staff; and they brought of the pomegranates, and of the figs.

The place was called the brook Eshcol, because of the cluster of grapes which the children of Israel cut down from thence.

And they returned from searching of the land after forty days.

And they went and came to Moses, and to Aaron, and to all the congregation of the children of Israel, unto the wilderness of Paran, to Kadesh; and brought back word unto them, and unto all the congregation, and shewed them the fruit of the land.

And they told him, and said, We came unto the land whither thou sentest us, and surely it floweth with milk and honey; and this is the fruit of it.

Nevertheless the people be strong that dwell in the land, and the cities are walled, and very great: and moreover we saw the children of Anak there.

The Amalekites dwell in the land of the south: and the Hittites, and the Jebusites, and the Amorites, dwell in the mountains: and the Canaanites dwell by the sea, and by the coast of Jordan.

And Caleb stilled the people before Moses, and said, Let us go up at once, and possess it; for we are well able to overcome it.

But the men that went up with him said, We be not able to go up against the people; for they are stronger than we.

And they brought up an evil report of the land which they had searched unto the children of Israel, saying, The land, through which we have gone to search it, is a land that eateth up the inhabitants thereof; and all the people that we saw in it are men of a great stature.

And there we saw the giants, the sons of Anak, which come of the giants: and we were in our own sight as grasshoppers, and so we were in their sight. (Numbers 13:1–33 KJV)

Free your thoughts from limitation. Your chance in life and your journey to greatness begins with a change in your thinking. The Bible says,

Whatsoever things are true, whatsoever things are honest, whatsoever things are just, whatsoever things are pure, whatsoever things are lovely, whatsoever things are of good report; if there be any virtue, and if there be any praise, think on these things. (Philippians 4:8 KJV)

Chapter 18

HOW TO BREAK OUT
OF LIMITATION

The Jabez prayer request example in the Bible is found in 1 Chronicles 4:9–10.

> Jabez was more honorable than his brothers. His mother had named him Jabez, saying, "I gave birth to him in pain." Jabez cried out to the God of Israel, "Oh, that you would bless me and enlarge my territory! Let your hand be with me, and keep me from harm so that I will be free from pain." And God granted his request. (NIV)

He was honorable and maybe behaved better than his brothers. His mother called him Jabez because she bore him with "sorrow or pain." When you look at the prayer he prayed, you can discover the problems he had.

Jabez wanted to be blessed by God. Jabez said, "Bless me indeed and enlarge my territory."

Was Jabez experiencing hardship? Was there certain lack of material things in his life?

God answered his prayer and granted him the desire of his heart.

Like Jabez, are we experiencing lack and limitation in our lives? Are we in pain or causing pain to others?

"Let Thine hand be with me" (1 Chronicles 4:10b NIV). Jabez could not see the hand of God on his life and what he was doing. He was probably experiencing failure in business, making wrong decisions, always losing money, or lacking favor because when the hand of God is on you, you will have direction and open doors.

> The second thing we learn about him is that, when he was born, his mother named him "Pain," or "Sorrow." That is a strange name to give to a newborn baby, but the mother's remark was, "I named him this because I bore him in sorrow, or pain." That remark could, of course, be referring to the pain of childbirth, but I doubt if that is what it means. If that were true, it would mean that every baby born in pain ought to be named "Jabez," so it would be the most popular name ever, if that were the case. Jabez had several brothers, we do not know how many, who were probably born in pain of childbirth too, but this indicates that something else was troubling the mother when Jabez was born. She was discouraged, she saw nothing ahead but hopeless difficulty, and she named the baby "Pain," or "Sorrow," because of that experience. (https://www.raystedman.org/thematic-studies/prayer/prayers-practicality)

In her book *The Real Blesser!*, Vivian Cynthia says, "We discover a man who moved beyond living a life of everyday blessing, to living a life of abundant blessing."

Jabez prays a simple prayer, totally according to God's will. His prayer went directly to the ears of God. God answered right away, and Jabez was blessed beyond measure.

Jabez prayed a model that God would bless him, increase his territory, place his hand upon him, and keep him from evil (1 Chronicles 4:10).

Jabez is distinctly remembered for what he prayed for and that God granted his request. Was Jabez possibly a man of faith? I am sure that from that day on, his pain was gone. Doors of opportunity suddenly were flung open before Jabez. He probably got new job offers and was able to buy land and increase his cattle. Jabez was blessed right in the midst of his pain, in front of his brothers and his neighbors who witnessed his pain.

In his book *Turning Your Mess into a Message*, Dr. Josef Howard writes, "His prayer became the casting distinction in his life to remove him from causing pain to being blessed by the hand of God."

Do you experience lots of pain in your life, like Jabez and his mother? God is just one prayer away. Call on him. He will answer you.

The Bible says,

> Call to Me and I will answer you, and I will show you great and mighty things, which you do not know. For thus says the LORD, the God of Israel, concerning the houses of this city and the houses of the kings of Judah, which have been pulled down *to fortify* against the siege mounds and the sword: 'They come to fight with the Chaldeans, but *only* to fill their places with the dead bodies of men whom I will slay in My anger and My fury, all for whose wickedness I have hidden My face from this city. Behold, I will bring it health and healing; I will heal them and reveal to them the abundance of peace and truth. And I will cause the captives of Judah and the captives of Israel to return, and will rebuild those places as at the first. I will

cleanse them from all their iniquity by which they have sinned against Me, and I will pardon all their iniquities by which they have sinned and by which they have transgressed against Me. Then it shall be to Me a name of joy, a praise, and an honor before all nations of the earth, who shall hear all the good that I do to them; they shall fear and tremble for all the goodness and all the prosperity that I provide for it. (Jeremiah (33:3–9 NIV)

It's strange the way that Jabez was introduced in this passage of Chronicles.

Then if you look a little closer, you will notice some omissions which are clues to what is going on. All through the chapter these other names are the names of heads of families [usually the great-grandfather and the father of a family will be introduced before the main character is introduced. Here] Jabez was introduced [suddenly] with no mention at all of his [ancestors]; no paternity, no inheritance, no heritage are mentioned. When you consider that these records in the Book of Chronicles were undoubtedly taken from the official registry of the temple … you realize that here is an official account of who was who in the land of Israel.

Jabez is introduced, however, not because of his father's name or anything about his father. Furthermore, it is evident from this account that there was a struggle going on in the family of Jabez. They seemed to be under the blight of terrible poverty, for Jabez prays, "Lord, enlarge my border," i.e., increase my material possessions. This indicates that something was amiss in this regard. Now when you remember that, in Israel, the land had been divided among the tribes and among the families by lot, that every family had its own inheritance which was passed on from generation to generation, you know that this inheritance was prized as being the great possession. (https://www.raystedman.org/ thematic-studies/prayer/prayers-practicality)

Again, we have to supply some of the details from our imagination. I cannot help but feel that Jabez's mother was probably a godly woman. You often find that kind of situation of a man who is blowing it, who is careless about his responsibility, living only for himself, yet he is married to a woman who stays at home, who tries to keep the family together, struggling valiantly against all the unhappiness and misery of poverty trying to teach her children something about God. At any rate, no matter where he learned this, Jabez learned that there was a God, and that he answered prayer. (https://www.raystedman.org/ thematic-studies/prayer/prayers-practicality)

Jabez prayed to God, "that thou wouldst bless me."

So what do we mean by it? Well, it seems to me that it is a request for some kind of an inner sense of relationship with God. "Blessing" is drawing near to God, finding him, knowing him personally. To be close to God, to walk with him, to share in his life, to know his Spirit, to be filled with his wisdom and to understand his loving, forgiving heart, all this is part of "blessing," and this is what Jabez is praying for. (https://www.raystedman.org/thematic-studies/ prayer/prayers-practicality)

God grants his request to him.

> Then second, Jabez prays, "Enlarge my border." This is a prayer for opportunity, for the restoration, in his case, of his lost inheritance, for a place to stand in the midst of the culture of his day in which he might gain some sense of status and respect. Translated into our own terms, it means to find a way to break out of whatever may be limiting us, hemming us in and enslaving us. Some of you may feel this because you are in the grip of some habit, some attitude of mind and heart. Some of you may feel that you are in a situation in which you have no opportunity to grow, to advance, to be fulfilled and satisfied. If that is the case, this is the proper kind of prayer to pray, "Lord, give me that opportunity. Let me find it. Open the door for me." Jabez prays that earnestly because of his lost inheritance. (https://www.raystedman.org/thematic-studies/prayer/prayers-practicality)

> Well, I am sure this is a prayer that comes naturally to his lips as he thinks of the uncertainty of the future he faces. All of us feel this way at times. We do not know what is coming down the road. We do not know what sudden, unexpected changes may occur in our lives in the next few days, months, or years. What we often want to ask for, therefore, is a revelation of what is coming, a glimpse ahead. (https://www.raystedman.org/thematic-studies/prayer/prayers-practicality)

> Now this is what Jabez is praying for: "Lord, be with me [1 Chronicles 4:10]. Go into the future with me.

Guide me that I may know that each step of the way I can trust the fact that you are with me, and if I need a touch of direction you will [guide me]." ...

Then the last request was, "Keep me from the evil so that it might not hurt me." I see in that request a deep awareness of a tainted heredity in this young man's life. Something he has inherited from his dissolute forebears has taken up residence in his own genetic makeup; he senses a weakness within that frightens him. I see this in many people. I feel it myself. It may be a tendency towards a hot temper, which destroys many opportunities that could be used for advantage, wrecked by a display of temper that turns everybody off and ruins everything. Maybe it is a lustful sexual life which constantly dwells on sexual themes so that the mind is continually bombarded with desires that race through the blood and awaken passions that ought to be subdued. Maybe it is avarice, some desire for the acquisition of material gain so that you will be safe and secure, have abundance, and do what you want. It is not for nothing that the Bible warns us, "The love of money is the root of all evil," (1 Timothy 6:10 KJV). Perhaps that is the weakness that is inside that Jabez fears. Whatever it was—and the text does not tell us—he knows that God is able to handle it. (https://www.raystedman. org/thematic-studies/prayer/prayers-practicality)

Let faith arise in your heart today. Start calling in the name of the Lord.

When you call on Jesus, you must have faith in your heart. Faith is the currency that you need to receive from God. You may be wondering, "How can I receive from this Jesus?" You need to be born again. In Matthew11:28, Jesus says, "Come unto me all ye that labor and are heavy laden and I will give you rest (NIV).

The Bible declares in Isaiah 59:20, "The Redeemer [Jesus] shall come to Zion and unto them that turn from transgression in Jacob" (KJV). Repent of your sins and confess with your mouth that Jesus died and rose again.

> Jesus answered and said unto him, Verily, verily, I say unto thee, Except a man be born again, he cannot see the kingdom of God. (John 3:3 KJV)

The Bible says,

> That if thou shalt confess with thy mouth the Lord Jesus, and shalt believe in thine heart that God hath raised him from the dead, thou shalt be saved. (Romans 10:9 KJV)

Chapter 19

PRAY THESE PRAYERS IN THE NAME OF JESUS

But thou Oh Lord art a shield for me, my glory and the lifter up of mine head. Oh Lord my God in the name of Jesus lift up my head from every flood of adversity in Jesus name. (Psalm 3:3 NIV)

Lift up your heads, O gates! And be lifted up, O ancient doors, that the King of glory may come in. Who is this King of glory? The LORD, strong and mighty, the LORD, mighty in battle. Every gate of limitation over my life, my family, my business or career life, family, my business and career, I smashed it in the name of Jesus! In the name of Jesus lift up your head. (Psalm 24:7–8 (KJV)

See, I am doing a new thing! Now it springs up; do you not perceive it? I am making a way in the wilderness and streams in the wasteland.

Every old structure that wants to limit my destiny from springing forth, it is written my God will make a way in the wilderness and rivers in the desert.

So you old structure of limitation in my life, in Jesus name collapse! (Isaiah 43:19 NIV)

He himself bore our sins in his body on the tree so that we might die to sins and live for righteousness, by his stripes we are healed. (1 Peter 2:24 NIV)

The theme of God's Word is man's Creation, man's Fall, and man's Redemption through Christ's Sacrificial Atoning Death on Calvary's Cross. However, it's interesting to note that Job's theme, if in fact it was the First Book of the Bible to be written, is not the conversion of a sinner, but the Sanctification of the Saint. The Holy Spirit wanted us to see what it takes to live for God. (https://www.donnieswaggart.org/articles/for-there-is-hope-of-a-tree)

Chapter 20

HOW TO DEVELOP A
RELATIONSHIP WITH GOD

It is perfectly possible to live an outwardly respectable life; to attend a place of worship Sunday by Sunday; and even to hold a position of leadership within the Christian church; and still to have missed this … truth [concerning] a personal relationship with God.

But it cheers us, too, to think that this is the Almighty God. (http://www.walkingwithgiants. net/sermons/he-restores-my-soul-a-sermon/).

He is all-knowing and searches all hearts and minds. He expectantly waits on us to come to his presence with worship, prayer, and praise. God does not "[lean over] the balcony of heaven and mocks us in our weakness" or wait to whack us in the head when we mess up. No, he is a loving God who "comes down to us, and dwells with us, as a loving father among his children, and as a caring shepherd among his sheep" (http://www.walkingwithgiants.net/sermons/ he-restores-my-soul-a-sermon/).

God wants to know you. God wants to be a friend to you. God wants to take care of you. God wants to bless you. God wants to heal you.

> Follow the great and first commandment in the law: love God with all your heart, soul, and mind. If you want to build a strong relationship with God, surrender yourself to Him. (https://inspiringtips.com/ways-to-strengthen-your-relationship-with-god)

Our primary purpose in life is to develop a relationship with God.

> You cannot truly love God if you don't know Him. Therefore, strengthen your connection with God by knowing Him better. You can know and understand God deeper by reading His words and teachings in the Scriptures, listening about Him from a true preacher, and practicing what you have learned from Him. (https://inspiringtips.com/ways-to-strengthen-your-relationship-with-god)

Trust God, pray, and read your Bible every day. Talk to God always. God will speak back to you.

Love your neighbor as yourself. Love your family.

These are the steps that will turn your situation around.

Printed in the United States
by Baker & Taylor Publisher Services